Anna Goes To Dance

Written by Julie A. Walker

Thank-you to Michelle Long, of Micki's Dance Connection in Brantford, ON, for use of the studio for this project, for many years of dance, and great memories. Thank-you to Anna's dance friends for their friendship and smiles, and her cousins Katelyn and Megan (pg.11), for unlimited lifts and balance fun!

AuthorHouse™ LLC
1663 Liberty Drive
Bloomington, IN 47403
www.authorhouse.com
Phone: 1-800-839-8640

©2014 Julie A. Walker. All Rights Reserved.

No part of this book may be reproduced, stored in a retrieval system, or transmitted by any means without the written permission of the author.

Published by AuthorHouse 01/22/2014

ISBN: 978-1-4918-3568-5 (sc)
978-1-4918-3569-2 (e)

Library of Congress Control Number: 2013921169

Any people depicted in stock imagery provided by Thinkstock are models, and such images are being used for illustrative purposes only. Certain stock imagery © Thinkstock.

This book is printed on acid-free paper.

Because of the dynamic nature of the Internet, any web addresses or links contained in this book may have changed since publication and may no longer be valid. The views expressed in this work are solely those of the author and do not necessarily reflect the views of the publisher, and the publisher hereby disclaims any responsibility for them.

This book is dedicated to Anna, a wonderful daughter, for her pure enjoyment of dance. May you always do what you enjoy.

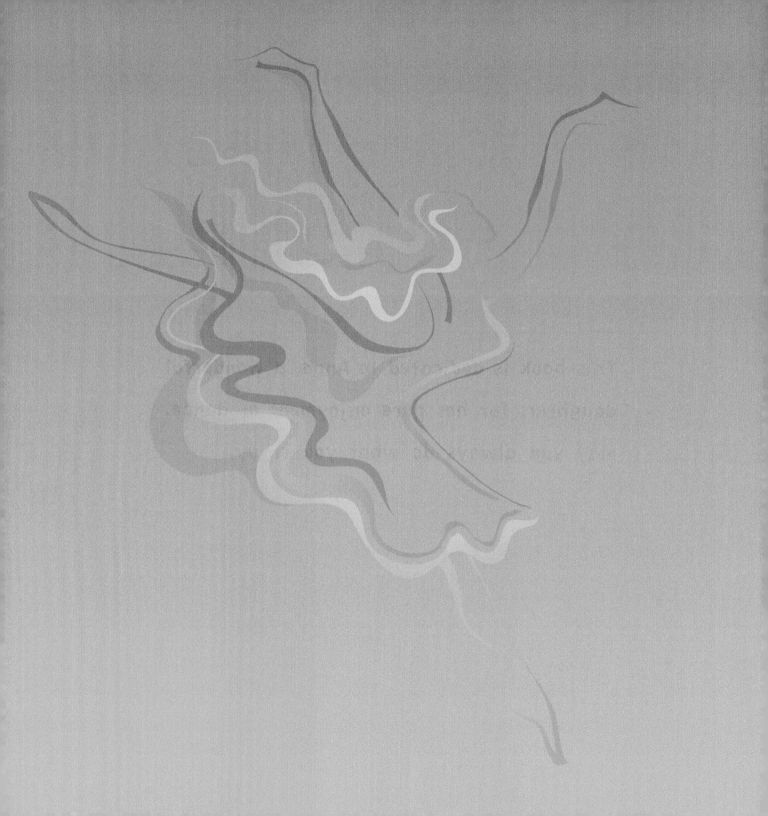

Table of Contents

Welcome to the studio 1

Jazz 4

Tap 6

Hip hop 8

Acro 10

Ballet 13

Costumes and Friends 20

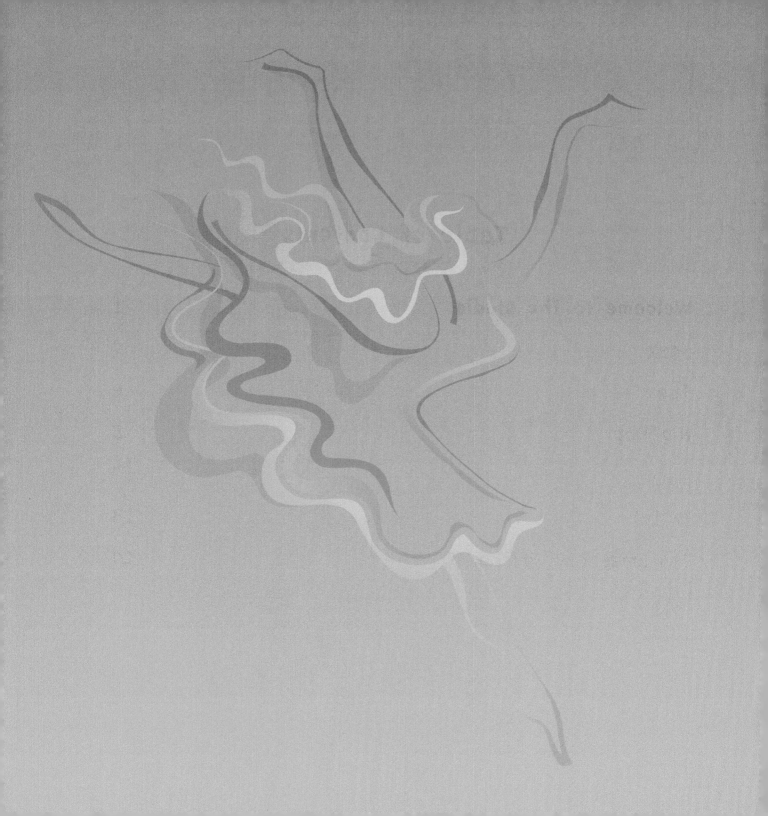

Hello! My name is Anna and I love to dance. I am learning many kinds of dance. I take lessons in jazz, tap, hip hop, acro, and ballet.

Dancing is so much fun! Lets go into my dance studio and I will show you what I do.

I have a locker in the change room where I can keep my dance clothes and shoes. I must hurry so I'm not late for class!

Today I begin by going to jazz class. I wear foot paws on the soles of my feet to help me turn. Some moves you may want to try are a step-hop, a needle, and splits.

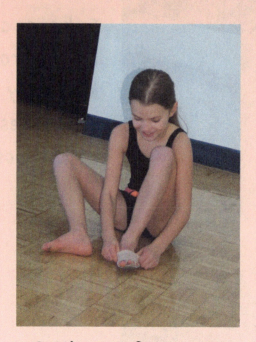

Putting on foot paws

Step-hop

Needle

Warming up

Splits

My favourite kind of dance is tap. I wear special shoes with metal taps on the bottom. I love the sounds I can make with my tap shoes.

Some of the first steps to learn in tap are shuffle, flap, and toe tap.

Another kind of dance is hip hop. Hip hop is fun and funky. I wear comfortable clothes and running shoes so I can groove to the music!

In hip hop class I like to do the shimmy, chug, and tornado!

If you like to dance but also love gymnastics, acro would be perfect for you! Acro is dance and gymnastics mixed together. Acro is fun because it has a lot of flips, cartwheels, and balances. I will show you some now, but remember to always stretch before you begin so you don't hurt your muscles.

Headstand

Balance

Cartwheel

Elbow stand

Now lets go to ballet. I began ballet when I was only one year old!

Look at me when I was younger...

As I grow, I get stronger and can learn more things.

Ballet is very important because it also helps me in all the other dances I learn. Ballet is very graceful and pretty to watch. I wear my hair in a bun and put on ballet tights, a body suit, and ballet shoes.

It is important to stretch at the start of any dance class.

Sometimes you hold the ballet barre to do exercises. You must always point your toes and stretch your legs.

There are five positions in ballet.
Let me show you them.

First

Second

Third

Fourth

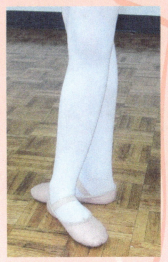
Fifth

Some other ballet moves are plié, which means to bend, and relevée, which means to rise up.

Ballet takes a lot of practice. I love it because it always makes me feel like a princess.

Learning new dance steps is great because my teacher can plan routines with many different moves in them. Once I know a new routine I practice it many times. Then I'm ready to wear my costume and perform on stage for an audience! Here are some of the costumes I have worn and great friends I have made.

Tap tap tap

Looking serious for hip hop!

Friends

Practicing for acro

After I have finished all of my classes I am tired, but I love dancing so much, I like to go home and practice some more! It is fun to make up my own dances to show my family and friends.

What I love most about dance are the nice friends I make. We have so much fun together! We are a dance team, working together to help each other do the best that we can.

Thank-you for sharing all of my dances with me. I hope you have learned some new dance moves! Don't forget, the most important thing to do when you are dancing is... SMILE!!

A special thank-you to big brother Cooper for many hours spent cheering on Anna and the MDC dance team!

CPSIA information can be obtained at www.ICGtesting.com
Printed in the USA
LVOW02s1907230414

382965LV00003B/7/P